W9-DAX-738

What Makes a ? Masterpiece?

HOUSES in Art

Words that appear in **bold** type are defined in the glossary on pages 28 and 29.

Please visit our web site at: www.garethstevens.com
For a free color catalog describing Gareth Stevens Publishing's
list of high-quality books and multimedia programs, call
1-800-542-2595 (USA) or 1-800-387-3178 (Canada).
Gareth Stevens Publishing's fax: (414) 332-3567.

Library of Congress Cataloging-in-Publication Data

Baumbusch, Brigitte.
    Houses in art / by Brigitte Baumbusch.
      p. cm. — (What makes a masterpiece?)
    Includes index.
    ISBN 0-8368-4381-9 (lib. bdg.)
    1. Buildings in art—Juvenile literature. I. Title. II. Series.
    N8217.B85B3813   2004
    704.9'44—dc22   2004045381

This edition first published in 2005 by
Gareth Stevens Publishing
A World Almanac Education Group Company
330 West Olive Street, Suite 100
Milwaukee, Wisconsin 53212 USA

Copyright © Andrea Dué s.r.l. 2001

This U.S. edition copyright © 2005 by Gareth Stevens, Inc.
Additional end matter copyright © 2005 by Gareth Stevens, Inc.

Translator: Erika Pauli

Gareth Stevens series editor: Dorothy L. Gibbs
Gareth Stevens art direction: Tammy West

Printed in the United States of America

1 2 3 4 5 6 7 8 9 08 07 06 05 04

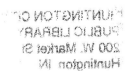

HOUSES
in Art

by Brigitte Baumbusch

GARETH**STEVENS**
GS
PUBLISHING
A World Almanac Education Group Company

What makes a house . . .

This "pink and yellow" picture is all houses.
Swiss artist Paul Klee painted it in 1919.

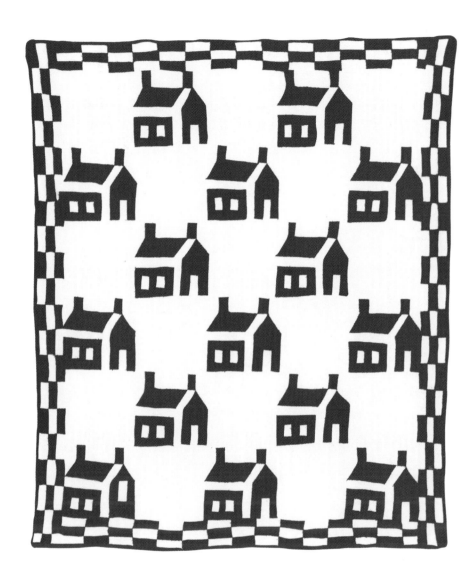

The patterns on this American quilt from the early 1900s are all **silhouettes** of simple houses. They were cut out of colored cotton cloth and sewn onto the quilt as **appliqués**.

a masterpiece?

Houses can look happy.

The small family in this drawing is enjoying a summer evening under a vine-covered **canopy**. The drawing was done with a brush. It was made by Japanese artist Kusumi Morikage more than three hundred years ago.

In this night scene, painted in the 1930s, American
artist Lyonel Feininger features dark apartment buildings
with lights on in only a few windows.

Houses can look sad.

Some houses are modern.

A **contemporary** Spanish artist named Josep Navarro Vives painted this brightly colored view of a modern city, with both large and small houses, in 1992.

This Egyptian country house, with a sycamore and a date palm at the front entrance, is very old. It was painted in a papyrus book more than 3,300 years ago. Papyrus is a plant the **ancient** Egyptians used to make a type of paper.

Some houses are ancient.

This is a house in summer.

This house on the shore of a lake is almost **engulfed** in summer plants. It was painted in Austria, early in the twentieth century, by Gustav Klimt, while he was on a summer vacation.

German artist Ernst Ludwig Kirchner painted this snow-covered mountain village in the 1920s. The art of that period, which was called "**Expressionism**," used strong outlines and colors, and the paintings were not always what the eye really saw.

These are houses in winter.

Houses can be scattered . . .

This **inlay** from the seventeenth century is made of colored stones. The artist used stones that already had the patterns he needed on them to make the hills and the sky. The inlay shows a typical **Tuscany landscape**. If you ever visit central Italy, you will, perhaps, see it there.

or crowded together.

This **medieval** city is a **fresco** painted seven centuries ago by the great Italian artist Giotto. Streets, then, were narrow, and the houses were all close to and on top of one another, with high walls around them for protection.

There are houses on water...

Some people live in houses that float on water. You can see one of these houses in the picture below. The painting is from 1874. The artist was an **Impressionist** painter named Claude Monet.

Gypsies are nomads, which means they are always on the move and have no permanent homes. Today, gypsies live in trailers, but in the past, they lived in **caravans**, like this one painted by Vincent van Gogh in the late 1800s.

and houses on wheels.

Some houses are made of terra-cotta...

This little painted **terra-cotta knickknack** is a model of a Mexican house from about 1,500 years ago.

This small **bronze** hut is really a container. The lid of the container is the roof of the hut. The container was made to look like one of the old houses found in Italy about 2,800 years ago.

others are made of bronze . . .

and some houses
are made of paper.

A contemporary artist in the United States made this paper house. The house looks as if it were made from a piece of folded paper, but it is actually a **collage** that **imitates** this effect. "Collage" is a French word that means "glued together."

This is a house of cards.

Building houses out of playing cards is a game that has been enjoyed by both young and old for many, many years. This group of children building a house of cards was painted in Russia, in the 1930s, by a woman who loved children.

Houses can be delicate porcelain . . .

This Chinese knickknack from the 1950s is a small **pagoda** made of brightly colored **porcelain**.

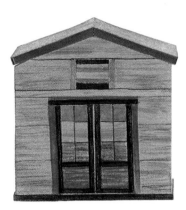

These little wooden houses are a Japanese toy.
One house fits inside the other, from smallest
to largest, just like a Russian **matryoshka**.

or sturdy wood.

Houses have windows . . .

A spacious room with large windows overlooks a breathtaking Italian landscape. It was painted by an English artist who lived in Italy in the 1920s.

through which to be seen...

This happy family group was painted in about the middle of the nineteenth century, in Germany. The young mother and her three children are seen through the window of their humble **peasant** house.

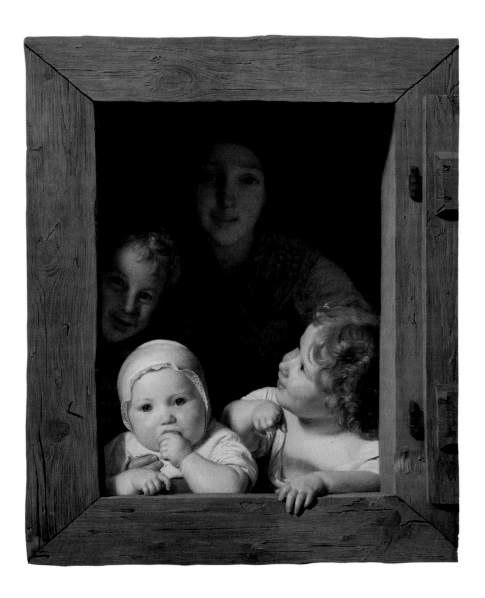

Two people are looking out a window at the birch woods outside their country house in Russia. This picture was painted by Marc Chagall in the early 1900s.

and out of which to look.

Houses have doors . . .

This doll house reproduces an English country cottage.
It was made in England in 1914.

for going out . . .

Although this fresco is painted on a solid wall, anyone looking at it might think that the little girl is really coming through the doorway.

Renaissance artist Veronese created the fresco **trompe l'oeil**, a French term meaning "fooling the eye." Trompe l'oeil paintings make you think you're looking at the real thing.

and for coming in.

GLOSSARY

ancient
relating to a time early in history, from the earliest civilizations until about the time of the Roman Empire

appliqués
shapes or designs that are cut out of fabric and attached to a larger piece of fabric for a decorative effect

bronze
a hard metal alloy (combination of two or more metals) that is a mixture of mainly copper and tin

canopy
a decorative awning or rooflike covering that overhangs an area, providing shelter or protection

caravans
groups of covered wagons, or other wheeled vehicles, traveling together in a line, one behind the other, like a train

collage
an art form that uses pieces of various materials, such as paper, fabric, wood, or metal, often in irregular shapes or sizes, arranging them to form a picture or a scene

contemporary
relating to a person or an event living or happening in current or modern times

engulfed
covered, submerged, or enclosed, as if being swallowed up or flowed over

Expressionism
an art movement of the early 1900s, promoting a style that sought to portray an artist's feelings or emotions about an object or event rather than a picture of the object or event itself

fresco
a painting on a wall; specifically, a type of painting that is typically done on fresh, damp plaster, using water-based paints or coloring

imitates
copies or tries to appear to be the same as something else

Impressionist
relating to a practice of French painters in the 1870s that gave subjects a more natural look by using strokes and dabs of primary colors to create the appearance or impression of actual reflected light

inlay
a scene or design made of decorative materials that are set into some kind of surface material

knickknack
a small, relatively insignificant, ornamental object, usually displayed just for decoration

landscape
a wide view of the natural scenery or land forms of a particular area that can be seen all at the same time from one place

matryoshka
a colorfully painted wooden doll, from Russia, with a series of progressively smaller dolls nestled inside

medieval
belonging to the Middle Ages, a period of history in Europe from the end of the Roman Empire to the 1500s

pagoda
an oriental tower, built mainly in the Far East to be used as a temple

peasant
relating to simple country life, often on a small, hand-worked farm

porcelain
a delicate white ceramic material used to make fine china dishes and figurines

Renaissance
a period of European history, between the Middle Ages (14th century) and modern times (17th century), during which learning flourished and interest in classical (relating to ancient Greek and Roman civilizations) art and literature was renewed, or "reborn"

silhouettes
basic outlines of figures that are cut out of a dark material, then are mounted on a light background

terra-cotta
brownish-orange earth, or clay, that hardens when it is baked and is often used to make pottery and roofing tiles

trompe l'oeil
a style of painting in which subjects are depicted in such a realistic way that they can "fool the eye" into seeing them as real

Tuscany
a region, or state, in northwestern Italy that is an important agricultural and industrial area as well as a center of art and learning

PICTURE LIST

page 4 — Paul Klee (1879-1940): Pink-yellow (Windows and Roofs), 1919. Munich, State Gallery of Modern Art. Photo Bayer & Mitko/Artothek. © Paul Klee by SIAE, 2001.

page 5— Pattern of houses for a cotton quilt. American folk art of the early 20th century. Private property. Drawing by Luigi Ieracitano.

page 6 — Kusumi Morikage (17th century): Enjoying the Evening Cool Under a Gourd Trellis, screen painted in ink and pale colors. Tokyo, National Museum. Drawing by Luigi Ieracitano.

page 7 — Lyonel Feininger (1871-1956): Lighted Apartment Houses, detail, 1932. Basle, Kunstmuseum. Photo Hans Hinz/Artothek. © Lyonel Feininger by SIAE, 2001.

page 8 — Josep Navarro Vives (20th century): City, 1992. Photo Contini Art Gallery, Venice. Reproduced by courtesy of the artist Josep Navarro Vives.

page 9 — Country house, detail from the Book of the Dead of Nakht. Egyptian art, late XVIII dynasty, c. 1350-1300 B.C., from Thebes. London, British Museum. Drawing by Luigi Ieracitano.

page 10 — Gustav Klimt (1862-1918): Kammer Castle on the Atter Lake (I), 1908. Prague, National Gallery. Photo Jochen Remmer/Artothek.

page 11 — Ernst Ludwig Kirchner (1880-1938): The Village of Monstein near Davos, 1927. Essen, Folkwang Museum. Photo Joachim Blauel/Artothek. © Ernst Ludwig Kirchner by Dr. Wolfang and Ingeborg Henze-Ketterer, Wichtrach, Bern, 2001.

pages 12-13 — Cigoli (1559-1613): Tuscan countryside, inlay in semi-precious stones. Florence, Opificio delle Pietre Dure. Photo Scala Archives.

page 13 — Giotto (1266-1336): Devils being driven from the city of Arezzo, detail of the city. From the fresco cycle of the Stories of Saint Francis. Assisi, Basilica of San Francesco. Photo Scala Archives.

page 14 — Claude Monet (1814-1926): Boat Atelier, 1874. Otterlo, Rijksmuseum Kröller-Müller. Photo Artothek.

page 15 — Vincent van Gogh (1853-1890): Les Roulottes (The Caravans). Paris, Museé d'Orsay. Photo Scala Archives.

page 16 — Polychrome terra-cotta model of a house. Nayarit culture, western Mexico, c. 100-500 A.D. Veracruz, Museum. Drawing by Sauro Giampaia.

page 17 — Hut urn in sheet bronze. Villanovan art, 8th century B.C., from Vulci. Rome, Museum of Villa Giulia. Drawing by Sauro Giampaia.

page 18 — Curtis Ripley (20th century): Page 487, detail, 1997, collage. Photo Modernism Gallery, San Francisco. © Modernism Gallery.

page 19 — Zinaida Serebriakova (1844-1967): Castle of Cards. Saint Petersburg, Russian State Museum. Photo Scala Archives.

page 20 — Glazed porcelain knickknack in the shape of a pagoda. Made in Ching-tao, China, in the 1950s. Private property. Drawing by Sauro Giampaia.

page 21 — Japanese painted wooden toy of the 20th century. Private property. Drawing by Sauro Giampaia.

pages 22-23 — Jessie Boswell (1881-1956): The Three Windows, 1924. Turin, Gallery of Modern Art. Photo Scala Archives.

page 24 — Ferdinand Georg Waldmüller (1793-1865): Young Peasant Woman with Three Children at the Window. Munich, Neue Pinakothek. Photo Blauel/Gnamm/ Artothek.

page 25 — Marc Chagall (1887-1985): Window in the Dacha. Moscow, Tretyakov Gallery. Photo Scala Archives. © Marc Chagall by SIAE, 2001.

page 26 — English doll house of the early 20th century. Private property. Drawing by Sauro Giampaia.

page 27 — Veronese (1528-1588): Little girl in the doorway, detail of the fresco decoration of a Venetian villa. Maser, Villa Barbaro. Photo Scala Archives.

INDEX